First published 2023

Seronands Publishing.

The right of Michelle Harverson to be identified as the author of this work has been asserted by her in accordance with the Copyright, Designs and Patents Act 1988.

All rights reserved. No part of this publication may be reproduced, stored in retrieval system, or transmitted, in any form, or by any means (electronic, mechanical, photocopying, recording or otherwise) without the prior written permission of the author. Any person who does any unauthorised act in relation to this publication may be liable to criminal proceedings and civil claims for damages.

Copyright © Michelle Harverson LLB (hons)

Dedication

Shades of Life is dedicated to everyone who just needs a little helping hand.

You are all stronger than you think.

Shades of Life

Authors Note

Some of the poems written are based on true events of others and include subjects' people may find distressing. They have been written with sensitivity and understanding free of judgement. My aim is that you will see there is hope in every situation as this theme runs throughout The Shades of Life.

To those that gave permission to write about your challenges through life – thank you. I hope I have done justice to the challenges you have faced.

To those who have chosen this book – thank you. Whatever your reasons for choosing, I hope that if you need help, you will reach out and ask.

Much Love.

Contents

The Shades of Life ... .10
Stars 11
Silent Tears ... .12
Strong Bonds ... .13
Love's Embrace ... .14
Silent Trauma ... .15
Rejections 16
Dance Through Life 17
Forgiving In Silence ... .18
Jumbled Mess ... .19
Unseen ... .20
The Rain ... .23
Silent Suffering ... .24
Road Less Travelled 25
Silently Living ... .26
Suffer Alone ... .27
Shattered Heart 28
The Magician 29
The Destroyer ... .30
Inspiration 31
Life is Short ... .32
Tomorrow ... .33
Shattered ... .34
Starry Night ... .35
Invasion ... .36
Wondrous Ride ... .37
Living Miserably ... .40
Inner Strength ... .41

Contents

Say 'Yes' 42
Let Go 43
Birth To Death 44
Loss Mum 45
Joyless Life 46
Crayons 47
The Streets 48
I Love You 49
Embrace 50
Secrets 51
Calorie Enemies 52
Poison 53
Another Life 55
Memories 56
The Girl 59
Darkness 61
We All Have a Story 62
It's Not Greener 63
Invisible Kiss 64
Trouble 66
Lost Voices 67
Already Enough 68
Death Row 69
Life's Journey 70
The Flame 71
Forever Changed 72
Yearning 73
Will To Survive 74
Apology 75

Contents

Unsafe Streets … ………………………78
A Deadly Game … ………………………80
Start Again … ………………………………81
Home ……………………………………………82
Triggers …………………………………………83
Fighting A War ……………………………84
Loss … ……………………………………………85
Amazing Things … ………………………86
Addiction … ……………………………………87
The Problem is You … …………………88
Trapped … ………………………………………89
Sounds Of Darkness … ………………90
Grudges … ………………………………………91
Stage 4 PTSD … ……………………………92
Scars … …………………………………………95
Deadly Substance ………………………96
A Life Not Yet Lived … …………………97
Sorry ……………………………………………98
Fear … ……………………………………………99
Secrets Lie … ………………………………100
Innocence Lost … ………………………101
The Road Ahead … ……………………102
Behind Closed Doors … ……………103
Believe in Yourself … …………………105
Overdose … ……………………………………106
Prescious Gem … …………………………107
Hiding … ………………………………………108
We Are Not Alone … ……………………109

Contents

Emptiness 110
Negative Thoughts 111
Intimacy 112
Homeless 115
It's A Trap 116
Narcissist 117
Night Terrors 118
Mental Torture 119
Treatment 120
Love 121
Age 122
Unplanned 123
Little Fighters 124
Head vs Heart 126
Sorrow 127
Triangle 128
Lotus Flower 129
Past Mistakes 130
Friendships 133
Change 134
Anorexia 135
Frustration 136
Women 137
The Storms Of Life 138
Shattered Glass 139
I'm Fine 140
Hope 141

Shades of Life

Life is like a rainbow
with shades of every hue,
some days are bright and sunny
while others are grey and blue.

There are moments of pure joy
and times of deep despair,
days when we feel like dancing
and moments when we just don't care.

Life is like a work of art
with colours bold and bright,
each brush stroke tells a story
and creates a unique sight.

So, embrace the many shades of life
and all the colours in between,
for it's the contrast and the diversity
that make the picture so serene.

Stars

Friends are like stars in the sky
they shine brightly as time goes by,
through thick and thin, they're always there
a constant presence, beyond compare.

They brighten up our darkest days
and guide us through life's many ways,
their laughter, love and endless support
are gifts that we should all exhort.

So, cherish your friends, like stars above
for their friendship is a treasure trove,
and just like the stars that light up the night
their love will shine forever bright.

Silent Tears

Silent tears fall down my face
a lonely ache I can't erase,
they speak of pain, they speak of sorrow
of all the things waiting on the morrow.

They speak of love, they speak of loss
of all the things that come at a cost,
they speak of dreams that have been shattered
of all the hopes that once all mattered.

Silent tears fall down my cheek
a language that I cannot speak,
they tell a story, they share a pain
of all the things that we can't explain.

Strong Bonds

Interwoven like vines on a trellis
our lives entwine, we cannot miss
the way we're bound, forever linked
a list of names, our hearts are synced.

Each person brings a unique thread
to this tapestry, we've finely bred
a pattern rich in diversity
a list of names, a true rarity.

And as we grow and journey on
our bonds remain, they're never gone
for we are part of something grand
a list of names, a sacred band.

Love's Embrace

In the dance of life, we intertwine
two beating hearts, beating in time,
our souls entwined, forever bound
in love's sweet embrace, we are found.

Hand in hand, we journey on
through life's twists and turns, we remain strong,
together we face each passing day
in love's warm glow, we find our way.

The bond we share, it knows no end
our love's a flame, that will transcend,
we'll dance and weave, through time and space
our love's sweet melody, we'll embrace.

Silent Trauma

In the face of silent trauma
women rise with strength and grace,
though their pain may be hidden
they refused to be erased.

They bear scars that none can see
yet they stand tall and proud,
their resilience and courage
are a testament to their crowd.

Through their struggles and their pain
they find their inner voice,
speaking out against injustice
they make a powerful choice.

So, let us celebrate these women
their spirit and their might,
for they are warriors who
overcome the darkest night.

Rejections

Rejections can be tough to take
leaving us feeling small and fake,
we put ourselves out there to see
if someone will accept the true me.

But when the answer is no
our confidence can take a blow,
we wonder what we did wrong
why we couldn't belong.

It's easy to feel alone
in a world that can be unknown,
but rejections are not the end
it's just a message to send.

We must keep trying and pushing through
believing in ourselves, and what we can do,
for rejection may hurt for a little while
but it's not enough to dim our shine.

Dance Through Life

Life is a dance, a rhythmic sway
a graceful movement day by day,
sometimes we twirl, sometimes we spin
sometimes we stumble and fall in.

We move to music, heard or unheard
with every step, a new sight to be explored,
we dance alone, we dance with friends
we dance through beginnings and through to the end.

Life is a dance, a beautiful art
a masterpiece created from the heart,
it's up to us to lead or follow
to embrace the rhythm and not be hollow.

So, take a step, and then take two
dance through life, with all that's true,
for in the end, what will remain
is the dance we danced in joy and pain.

Forgiving in Silence

Forgiving in silence is a powerful act
a choice to release the anger and pact,
to let go of hurt and move on with grace
and not let resentment take up space.

It's not about forgetting or excusing the wrong
but freeing oneself from bitterness so strong,
to find peace in the midst of pain and strife
and choose to live a more abundant life.

Forgiving in silence may not be easy
but it's a step towards healing that's worthy,
it allows one to let go and start anew
and find a brighter path to pursue.

So, let us practice forgiveness in our hearts
and let compassion and love play their parts,
for in forgiving we set ourselves free
and find true joy and serenity.

Jumbled Mess

My thoughts collide like a messy room
each idea fighting for its own space,
a cluttered mind, a chaotic gloom
where concentration is hard to embrace.

Words and phrases swirl around
like a whirlwind in my head,
a jumbled mess, no sense is found
as I try to sort them out instead.

But sometimes in the midst of the mess
a spark of inspiration ignites,
and from the chaos, I can address
a new idea that takes flight.

So, I'll embrace the cluttered mind
and all the chaos it may bring,
for within it, new thoughts I'll find
and inspiration will take wing.

Unseen

Silently we move through life
like ships sailing in the night,
guided by stars up above
towards a destination out of sight.

We face the winds of change
and the storms that come our way,
but we navigate through them all
and continue day by day.

Though we may feel alone
in this journey that we take,
we are surrounded by others
who also navigate this same lake.

So, let us be kind and compassionate
as we silently go through life,
for we never know the struggles
that others face in their strife.

'You can only win, when your mind is stronger than your feelings'

The Rain

The rain falls softly
washing away our woes,
it cleanses the earth
and refreshes our souls.

Each drop a reminder
that troubles can be washed clean,
as the rain falls silently
it offers a chance to begin again.

Let the rain wash away
all that burdens your heart,
feel the peace it brings
as it washes your troubles apart.

So, let the rain fall down
and let is wash your worries away,
embrace the cleansing power
and let it brighten your day.

Silent Suffering

Silent suffering is a heavy burden to bear
enduring pain alone, with no-one to share,
a smile on the face, but inside a broken heart
hiding the struggle, playing the part.

In silence, tears fall like rain
but no-one sees the hidden pain,
the world moves on, oblivious and unaware
of all the anguish and despair.

Yet, there is strength in the quiet fight
a resilience that shines through the darkest night,
for in the depths of the soul, there is a flame
that burns bright, despite the pain.

So, if you're suffering in silence today
know that you are not alone on your way,
there is hope, there is light at the end
a listening ear, a helping hand, a friend.

Road Less Travelled

The road less travelled
is the one we often fear,
but it's the path that leads us
to a future bright and clear.

It's easy to follow the crowds
and go where others go,
but the road less travelled
is where the magic flows.

It may be rough and bumpy
and at times you'll feel alone,
but the journey is worth it
for the treasures that are shown.

So, take a step forward
on the path that's not well known,
for the road less travelled
is where you'll find your own.

Silently Living

Silently living
invisible to the crowd,
homeless people
their fate so loud.

No place to call home
no bed to rest their head,
the street lights their domain
a life of constant dread.

Day after day
they struggle to survive,
their needs so basic
yet hard to derive.

Some may judge
without knowing their pain,
but who are we
to make assumptions in vain.

Let's open our hearts
and lend a helping hand,
for in the end
we should try and understand.

Suffer Alone

We secretly hurt and silently cry
behind the smile, we try to hide,
the pain and sorrow we keep inside
we suffer alone, with no-one to confide.

Our tears flow like a river at night
as we struggle to put up a decent fight,
against the demons that haunt our mind
and the memories that leave us all just blind.

We long for someone to understand
to hold our hand and help us stand,
but we fear the judgement and rejection
so, we keep our pain secret and hidden.

But know that you are not alone
there are others too, who feel like a stone,
reach out and let your voice be heard
for healing begins with a single word.

Shattered Heart

My heart shattered into a million pieces
as I watched the love of my life walk away,
I'm lost and alone in a world full of creases
struggling to find a reason to live each day.

I used to have purpose, a drive, a goal
but now I'm aimless drifting in the wind,
I feel like I'm stuck in a deep, dark hole
unable to climb out, unable to begin.

The pain is overwhelming, the tears won't stop
I wish I could turn back time and make it right,
but life goes on and I must find a way to cope
to heal my shattered heart and find the light.

Maybe one day I'll find purpose again
and the pieces of my heart will mend and grow,
until then, I'll keep moving forward my friend
and let the winds of change help me to flow.

The Magician

Our mind plays tricks on us
a magician with hidden powers,
it creates illusions and fantasies
bringing us joy or causing us to cower.

The past and future it can distort
making us believe what isn't true,
anxiety and fear it may exhort
leaving us feeling blue.

Yet amidst the chaos and confusion
our mind can also bring clarity,
it holds the key to our solution
unlocking our potential with charity

So, let us embrace our mind
with all its tricks and quirks,
for it is the greatest treasure we can find
a gift that forever works.

The Destroyer

Paranoia, the destroyer
wreaks havoc on the mind,
twisting thoughts into monsters
that are impossible to unwind.

Suspicion becomes a constant
and trust is lost in every face,
the world becomes a prison
and escape is a hopeless chase.

Sleep is just a fleeting dream
as the mind races on and on,
searching for threats and dangers
until the break of dawn.

Paranoia, the destroyer
tears apart what we hold dear,
leaving behind a hollow shell
of what used to be so near.

Inspiration

In every moment, an opportunity lies
to find inspiration and let it rise.
A simple word or a fleeting glance
can spark a flame, a creative dance.

Life is Short

Life is short, we often hear
in the blink of an eye, it can disappear,
so let us cherish every moment we hold dear
and make the most of our time whilst we are here.

We may not know what the future holds,
but we can choose how our story is told,
with every decision, our destiny unfolds
so, let's make each one count, be brave and bold.

Life may be fleeting, but it's also sweet
filled with love, laughter and people we meet,
let's savour each moment, embrace the heat
and live our lives with passion and heartbeat.

For when our time comes, as it inevitably will
let us leave behind a legacy that lingers still,
of a life well lived with love that spills
and memories that warm hearts and souls until.

Life is short, but it's also beautiful and bright
let's make the most of it, with all our might,
and live everyday like it's our last flight
with love, joy and courage, shining like a light.

Tomorrow

Tomorrow never comes
it's always out of reach
we live for today
and the lessons it can teach.

We plan and dream
of what could be instore
but the future's uncertain
and tomorrows not guaranteed anymore.

So, lets cherish this moment
and make the most of today
for tomorrow may never come
and yesterday has already slipped away.

Shattered

A shattered mind, a fractured soul
the pieces scattered, beyond control,
the thoughts that once were clear and bright
now twisted, warped and out of sight.

The memories that once brought joy
now cause pain that can't be ignored,
the voices in the head won't cease
a never-ending cycle of inner peace.

The broken mind can't be fixed
no matter how hard it's tried and mixed,
but hope remains, a glimmer of light
that someday the pieces will reunite.

Starry Night

In the starry night
the sky shines so bright
a canvas of black
with stars to attract.

The moon shines so clear
with a glow that's sincere
a guide in the night
for travellers in sight.

The stars twinkle and gleam
like a beautiful dream
a sight to behold
with stories untold.

In the starry night
the universe takes flight
a wonder to see
for you and me.

Invasion

You invaded my personal space
and now you occupy my mind
moon filled skies, leave me restless
as my thoughts turn cold and dazed.

A momentary lapse of your judgement
raises memories from the past
chapters of life which were closed
rear their ugly head - *how sad*

The uphill battle continues
to regain my mental strength
if only you had restrained yourself
instead of hiding behind your mental health.

Wondrous Ride

Life is a journey with twists and turns
a path that we each much traverse,
sometimes we stumble, sometimes we learn
and sometimes we feel like we're just cursed.

But through it all, we gain perspective
and see the world in a different light,
our struggles and pain become instructive
and we emerge from the darkness, shining bright.

For life is a gift, a precious treasure
and each day is a chance to grow,
we can choose to focus on the pressure
or dwell on the hardships we know.

So, let us embrace the wondrous ride
and cherish every moment we're given,
for life is a joy that we can't hide
a blessing that makes our hearts driven.

'The bravest thing I ever did was continue my life when I wanted to die – *and nobody really knows'*

Living Miserably

Living miserably is a terrible fate
a life devoid of joy, full of hate,
everyday feels like a never-ending fight
and happiness is nowhere in sight.

But why should we suffer in this way?
instead, we should not let misery rule the day.
life is too short to waste on despair
so, lets live with love and not with fear.

We can find love in the smallest of things
and joy in the happiness that life brings,
let's cherish each moment, and make it count
and never let our happiness be held down.

So, let's lift our heads up and face the sun
and leave behind our misery, once and for all,
let's choose to live a life that's full and bright
and make the most of every moment in sight.

Inner Strength

In the depths of our being
lies a strength so profound
a force that keeps us going
when life's challenges abound.

Our inner strength is steadfast
a flame that never dies
it guides us through the darkness
and lift's us to the skies.

It's born of our experiences
our triumphs and our pain
it's nurtured by our courage
and our willingness to sustain.

So, when life's storms are raging
and we feel we're at our end
remember our inner strength
and the power to transcend.

For within us lies a hero
a warrior filled with light
and with our inner strength
we can conquer any fight.

Say 'Yes'

Saying yes to life is a beautiful thing
an adventure that is forever unfolding
it means taking risks, trying new things
and embracing all the joy that life can bring.

Being a yes person means living without fear
and letting go of all that holds us back
it means saying yes to opportunities near
and never letting courage slack.

For every yes is a chance to grow
to learn and discover what we didn't know
it means taking a leap of faith
and trusting that we'll find our way.

So, say yes to life, and all its endless wonder
and let your spirit soar and thunder,
for in saying yes, we find our true selves
and live a life that's rich and never dull.

Let Go

In the midst of chaos and the rush of life
there lies a place of peace, free from strife
it's found within, a tranquil space
That fills the soul with gentle grace.

No need to search the world around
for what we seek is already found
the key to unlock this peaceful door
is to look within and seek no more.

Let go of worries and let them fade
as you close your eyes and breathe in shade
feel the calmness spread within
as you let go of all that's been.

In this serene and tranquil state
the mind is clear, and the worries abate
a sense of peace that fills the heart
a place where all our troubles depart.

So, take a pause and find this place
of inner peace and gentle grace
for its within us that we find our way
to a life that's peaceful every day.

Birth to Death

Life is a gift, a precious treasure
a journey that we all must measure
each day a new opportunity
to see the beauty of diversity.

From birth to death, we walk this earth
experiencing joy, pain and mirth
we learn and grow with each passing day
and cherish the moments along the way.

Life is a gift, to be cherished and savoured
with each breath we take, our soul is flavoured
we find our purpose, and live with intention
and make the most of every situation.

So, let us embrace this gift we've been given
and live each day like it's a slice of heaven
for life is a gift, a treasure to behold
a journey to cherish, a story to be told.

Loss Mum

Losing a child is a pain beyond measure
a wound that can never truly be healed
it's a life sentence that we cannot treasure
a fate that we never thought would be sealed.

As a loss mum, we carry a heavy load
our hearts are forever broken and scarred
we walk through life on an uncertain road
with memories of our child forever charred.

We long to hold them, to feel their embrace
to hear their laughter and see their smile
but all that's left is an empty space
a void that no words can reconcile.

Yet through the pain, we find a way to cope
to honour their memory and keep them near
we carry them with us and never lose hope
that someday we'll hold them again, so dear.

So, to all the loss mums out there, know this
you are not alone in this journey of grief,
together we'll find a way to persist,
and find comfort in the memories we keep.

Joyless Life

Sadness fills my mind, a joyless life
a constant weight, a never-ending strife
the world around me seems so bleak
everyday just feels like another defeat.

The sun may shine, but I can't feel its warmth
my heart is heavy, my soul is worn
I long for happiness, for a glimmer of light
but it feels like I'm trapped in an endless night.

My tears fall like rain, a never-ending stream
and I wonder if this is all just a bad dream
I try to shake it off, to find some hope
but it feels like I'm at the end of my rope.

Yet still I hold on, to what, I don't know
maybe my sadness will let go
until then I'll keep holding on
and hope that one day I'll see the dawn.

Crayons

Life is like a box of crayons
each colour represents a shade
some bright and bold, others more subdued
but all important in their own way.

Like crayons, life can be messy
with lines that sometimes go astray
but with each stroke and every mark
our unique masterpiece takes shape.

We may not always have every colour
and sometimes we must make do
but it's the combination of hues and tones
that create a beautiful view.

So, embrace the colours of life
and let your true colours shine through
for in this box of crayons we call life
there's a masterpiece waiting for you.

The Streets

Amidst the concrete jungle, they roam,
their homes are the streets, they call their own
with nothing much to call their own
they brave the harshness of the unknown.

Their strength is like no other
enduring the cold and their hunger
they face life's challenges head on
with every sunrise, a new dawn.

Their spirit remains unbroken
their will to survive unspoken
they persevere through each day
with hope in their hearts to pave the way.

The homeless have a story to tell
of resilience and strength that compel
their struggles may be great and many
but their spirit shines like a brand-new penny.

So, let us not forget them in our midst
for they are warriors in the own right
may we give them the respect they deserve
and the support they need to survive the fight.

I Love You

Speak now, don't wait
for time is never late
the words you hold inside
could be your greatest fate

Say 'I love you' with all your heart
and let your feelings start
for love is meant to be shared
and not kept apart.

Speak now, don't hesitate
for tomorrow may be too late
regret is a heavy weight
that you don't want to take.

So, take a chance and speak your mind
for life is short and time is kind
the words you say could change a life
and bring you joy to those in strife.

Speak now, don't hold back
for courage is what you lack
the words you say could be the key
to set your spirit free.

Embrace

Life is too short to waste a day
to let our dreams just slip away
we must seize each moment, every chance
and embrace the world with a fearless stance.

Life is too short to hold onto hate
to let bitterness determine our life and fate
we must forgive and learn to love
and soar beyond the clouds like a dove.

Life is too short to shy from the unknown
to stay within our comfort zone
we must explore and take the leap
and trust that the path we seek, will keep.

Life is too short to simply exist
to merely survive, to never persist
we must live with passion in our heart
and leave a legacy that sets us apart.

So, let us make the most of today
and never let our spirit sway
for life is too short to waste away
and we have a chance to make it great.

Secrets

In the stillness of the night
when the world is fast asleep
my thoughts drift to you, my dear
and the love I secretly keep.

Reflections of your smile
and the way your laughter rings
echoes in my heart and mind
as I think of all these things.

I know I cannot tell you
of the love that I hold true
but in my heart, you'll always be
my one and only muse.

So, in the stillness of the night
as I lay me down to sleep
I'll dream of you my dear
and the love I secretly keep.

Calorie Enemies

I can see it in your eyes
that burning desire to be thin
you'll do whatever it takes
to have the perfect body that's in

You count your calories
and spend hours at the gym
and push yourself to the limit
and your efforts never dim

But perfection is elusive
and beauty is in the eye of the beholder
don't let society's standards
make you feel like you're not bolder.

Embrace your curves and imperfections
and love yourself as you are
your worth is not determined
by a number on a scale or a superficial bar.

So, don't chase after a mirage
and don't let perfection consume you
you are beautiful just the way you are
and that's all you need to pursue.

Poison

When we think of poison
what springs to mind
is it the arsenic, mercury, gases or strychnine.

For me, poison is ultimately different
it's in the loss of hair
the pale white skin
the lack of energy
the self-doubt within

the poison is what's saving lives
the unspoken treatment
that so often deprives.

They tell us it's a miracle
the treatment works like magic
but the reality of being poisoned
has too many effects, it's tragic.

The cancer may be gone
people see you getting better
but they do not understand
the effects that remain and linger.

The everlasting damage
cancer treatment takes on you
it's hard to be constantly grateful
for a life that's now renewed.

It's the words that no-one speaks
because we're supposed to be always happy
but for far too many people
it is now their only reality.

Another Life

They say a cat has nine lives
But what if we had another?

In my second life, I would wander from country to country, eating and drinking, living free.
I would breathe the crisp air of mountains and feel the soft white sands between my toes.
I would buy a little house by the lake, filled with books, so many books and a log fire roaring with flame.

Perhaps I would have a man, just for the weekend, fleeting visits so I could remain free to roam the world.
Perhaps I would love, but not the man, maybe myself, as self-worth and self-esteem grows beyond all else.

The second life would be an adventure, but not of loneliness, of power and belief that we can live on our terms, no one else's.

Memories

In the depths of the night, I lay awake
my mind consumed by past mistakes
the memories haunt, they never fade
and in my heart, the pain, it stayed.

The trauma of what once occurred
a weight upon my soul incurred
the sleepless nights are all too real
as I try to escape and to heal.

But still they come, the thoughts and fears
a flood that's lasted all these years
yet still I strive to find some peace
and from this darkness find release.

So, I hold on, and I endure
and pray that someday I'll be sure
that I can lay my past to rest
and finally find some sweet, sweet rest.

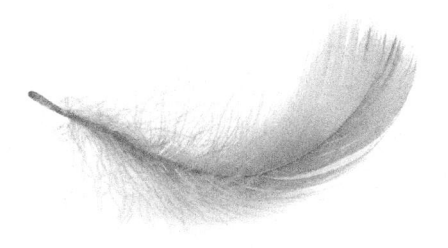

'Everyone has the opportunity to be young, but not everyone is fortunate enough to get old – *so enjoy life*'

The Girl

She was the girl from the roughest council estate
the girl who was under child protection
the girl that fought her way through life
the girl who got constant rejection.

She was the girl
who constantly ran away
the girl that was quiet
and never wanted to stay

She was the girl
that said enough was enough
who made a stand
when things got rough

She's now the woman
who educated herself
who strives for great things
despite issues with health

She's now the woman
who always has a voice
strongest of all
millionaires' status to rejoice.

She's now the woman
helping so many others
educate, achieve, believe
those that don't have mothers.

Darkness

In the silence of my room at night
I feel a sense of heartfelt fright
as I lie here all alone
my heart just feels like a heavy stone.

The world outside seems too far away
as I struggle to find the words to say
the ache inside me is hard to bear
as I long for someone to just be there.

But in the darkness, I find peace
as my thoughts and feelings start to release
I know that I am not truly alone
for my heart has a place to call its own.

So, though I may feel lonely at times
I know that my heart will always chime
with the rhyming sound of love and hope
guiding me through life's endless scope

We all Have a Story

We all have a story
a tale to be told
of the joys we've experienced
and the hardships we've known.

Sometimes we wear them
on our sleeves for all to see
but often they're hidden
as deep as they can be.

So, let us be kind
for we never truly know
the struggles and the battles
that others undergo.

May empathy and compassion
be the guiding lights we share
and may we always remember
that each story deserves care.

For in our human journey
we all need love and grace
so, let us be kind to one another
and create a better place.

It's not Greener

The grass is not always greener on the other side
for comparison is a thief that steals our pride
we look at what others have with envious eyes
but fail to see the blessings in our own lives.

The grass may seem greener, lush and bright
but we don't know the struggles hidden from sight
we compare our worst to others best
and in doing so, we rob ourselves of rest.

Let us learn to appreciate what we have
and not be consumed by what we lack
for the grass may not be greener on the other side
but we can make our own grass greener with pride.

Invisible Kiss

An invisible kiss
so light and so sweet
it lands on your cheek
and makes your heart, beat.

It comes from afar
from love that's so true
it's a secret that's kept
just between me and you.

No-one else can see it
it's just for us two
an invisible symbol
of the love that we pursue.

So, close your eyes tight
and feel it on your skin
that invisible kiss
that lets you know we'll win

For love like this
so pure and so bright
can conquer all obstacles
and make everything right.

So, lets cherish this kiss
and keep it alive
for it's a symbol of love
that will always survive.

Trouble

I knew you were trouble when I first met you
your eyes were like fire, your smile so untrue
you had a way of charming, but I saw through
the lies and the games, the things you would do.

You said all the right things, but they were all wrong
you led me on, then left me alone.
I should have known better, not to fall so fast
but your spell was too strong, I couldn't last.

Now here I am, picking up the pieces
of a heart that your broke, with your loveless releases
but I would let you win, I'll rise above
and find a love that's real, built on trust and love.

Lost Voices

Keeping feelings inside can be a heavy burden to bear,
a weight on your heart that's hard to share
it may seem easier to hide what's within
But the truth is, it only adds to the din.

The world around us can be so loud
that our own voices get lost in the crowd
it's easy to believe that no-one cares
that our feelings are too much to bear.

But the truth is, we all feel this way
at some point in time, on some given day
so, don't keep your feelings locked up inside
share them with someone, let them be your guide.

For when we open up and let others in
we find that we're not alone in our sin
we can heal and grow and find our way
and our feelings can help us seize the day.

Already Enough

It is easy to fall into the trap of believing that we are not enough.
The world around us often seems to reinforce this belief, with messages that we need to be more successful, more attractive, more accomplished.

But the truth is, we are already enough – ***just as we are***

Death Row

On death row, I sit and wait
for my final and ultimate fate
I ponder on the life I've had
and all the things that I have said.

Regret and sorrow fill my heart
for all the people I did harm
if only I could turn back time
and make amends for all my crimes.

But now it's too late for that
my actions have led me to this path
I take responsibility for my deeds
and hope that my soul will find peace.

As I wait for the final call
I pray that God forgives all
and that my loved ones can move on
after I'm gone and my life is done.

Life's Journey

Life is a journey with twists and turns
changes that we face, sometimes unearned.
a constant evolution, a never-ending flow
we must adapt, for that's how we grow.

From the first steps we take, to the last breath we make
life's changes shape us, make us who we are today.
the winds of change can be harsh, they can be kind
but we must keep moving forward, with an open mind.

Some changes bring joy, some bring pain
but we must keep going, with hope in our hearts to sustain
for every change, there's an opportunity to learn
to grow, to evolve, to better discern.

So, embrace the changes, let them be your guide
for they are what makes your journey all worthwhile
and when you reach the end of this ride
May you know that you've lived with style.

The Flame

Love is a flame that burns so bright
it brings a warmth in the coldest nights
but with its heat, comes a warning
for love can leave our hearts in mourning.

It starts as a spark, small and bright
a flicker of hope in the darkest night
but as it grows, it consumes us whole
burning away all, we know.

Love consumes us like a wildfire
burning everything, it touches with desire
but when the flame dies down, we're left with ash
wondering how something so beautiful could
ultimately crash.

So be careful with the love you hold
for it can leave you feeling rather cold
but if you tend to it with loving care
love can be a flame that's rare.

Forever Changed

I wonder if I should thank you
or if I should just hate you
what you did all those years ago
made the world lose all its glow.

It left me forever changed
a child with no answers – completely unexplained.
cold and alone
with a child of my own.

But you underestimated me
and the power I possess
the queen that I turned into
no longer in distress.

You made me grow up faster
than any child should have too
but thanks to you, I am now
better, taller, stronger.

Yearning

Waiting in hope to see you
feels like an endless trial
my heart beats with anticipation
like a bird longing to take flight.

Every moment feels like a lifetime
as I long for your embrace
my soul is filled with yearning
to gaze into your loving face.

The days tick by so slowly
and my patience wears so thin
but I hold onto hope
that soon you'll be with me

Until that day arrives
I'll wait with steadfast faith
for the moment when we'll be together
and my heart will no longer ache.

Will to Survive

When life throws hurdles in our way
and we're left feeling lost and astray
it's the will to survive that keeps us going
even when the winds of change are blowing.

Though the road may be long and tough
and the path ahead may seem rough
we dig deeper and find strength within
and keep pushing, despite the din.

For the will to survive is a peaceful force
that helps us weather any storm of course
it gives us the grit to keep moving forward
and the resilience to stand tall, never cornered.

So, let us embrace the will to survive
and let it help us thrive not just survive
for with it, we can conquer any trial
and emerge victorious with a smile.

Apology

We owe ourselves an apology
for the times we didn't believe
in our strength and ability
and let our doubts deceive

We owe ourselves an apology
for the times we put ourselves last
and let others needs take priority
ignoring our own needs so fast.

We owe ourselves an apology
for the times we didn't speak our truth
and let others' opinions rule
silencing our own voice, uncouth.

But now it's the time to make amends
to ourselves, our own best friend
to believe in our power within
and let our own light shine and bend.

So, let us forgive ourselves for the past
and focus on the present and future bright
let's give ourselves the love that lasts
and live our lives with all our might.

**A wound is a place
where light enters you.**

**Let it in, let it shine, for only when we shine, can
we –** *truly begin to heal.*

Unsafe Streets

In the darkness of the night
she wept alone, out of sight
her heart heavy with pain and sorrow
the wounds inflicted by a heart so hollow.

She walked the streets all on her own
for a man to follow unbeknown
what he did cannot be written
but the pain that followed, remains always hidden.

She tried to hold on, to make it right
but he took pleasure in her plight
her tears where his only delight
the bruises a mark of his plight.

But she rose from the ashes
her spirit unbroken, she dashes
towards a future, bright and bold
a little of happiness, she now holds.

For though the scars may never heal
she found the strength to break the seal
of silence, of fear, of oppression
and now she stands tall, in her own expression.

She is a woman strong and true
and though mistreated
and sometimes blue
she is a warrior, through and through.

A Deadly Game

Overdose, a deadly game
a risk too great, a life to claim
a moment of pleasure, a lifetime of pain
a tragic end, a life in vain.

The heart slows down, the breath grows weak
the mind fades away, the body too meek
a life cut short, a future undone
a loved one lost, a battle un-won.

Let us spread awareness, let us take a stand
let us lend a hand, to those in demand
let us fight this epidemic, let us end this strife
let us save them and give back their life.

Start Again

If I could start life again
I'd live it with more zest
I'd cherish every moment
and strive to do my best.

I'd take more time to listen
to the whispers of my heart
I'd be true to myself
and make a brand-new start.

I'd learn from my mistakes
and let go of all my fears
I'd embrace each new challenge
and wipe away my tears

I'd love with all my heart
and hold nothing back
I'd be kind to all I meet
and never lose track

If you could start life again
would you live with no regret
for every path you've taken
has brought you here, don't forget.

Home

Home is where the heart is
or so I am told,
but what if our hearts are broken
do we still have a place to call home.

It's where we share our laughter
and where we shed our tears
it's where we find our solace
and where we face our fears.

Home is where the heart is
a place of warmth and light
it's where we find our purpose
and where our souls take flight.

So, cherish your home and loved ones
and hold them close each day
for home is where the heart is
and it's where we long to stay.

Triggers

Triggers can come in many forms
the sights, the smells, the sounds, the norms,
a feeling, a place, a certain date
bringing back memories we try to abate.

PTSD triggers can strike at any time
bringing up memories that seem like a crime
the past rushes in like a tidal wave
making it hard to be present and brave.

Flashbacks, nightmares and panic attacks
we try to fight them, but they keep coming back
the triggers remind us of what we've been through
and all the pain we've had to push through.

But we're not alone in this fight
we can reach out and hold on tight
to those who understand and can relate
and help us navigate this difficult state.

PTSD triggers may be tough to bear
but with support, we can learn to repair
and find a way to live and thrive
even with the memories that still survive.

Fighting a War

Battling illness is like fighting a war
a battle fought on an internal shore
the body and mind endure the pain
as they fight to remain on the terrain.

The enemy within, it takes its toll
as it tries to take over the soul
but the spirit within is strong and true
and it fights with all its might to pull through.

Doctors and nurses lend a helping hand
as they guide the way to a better land
friends and family offer their love and care
as they stand by to help with each despair.

The battle may seem long and hard
but with each day, strength is marred
and as the sun rises high above
hope springs external with a sense of love.

So, keep fighting dear warrior of light
for victory is within your sight
and when the battle is finally won
you'll emerge stronger, with the battle done.

Loss

Loss is a weight that no-one should bear
it's a pain that we all must learn to share
the tears that fall from our eyes
are a reminder of the love that never dies.

The memories we hold so dear
are like a balm to the wounds we fear
the laughter we shared with those we lost
is the legacy that comes at such a cost.

For loss is a burden that we must bear
but it's also a reminder that love is there
love that never fades or dies
and that's the comfort that comes from goodbyes.

Amazing Things

When we let the world dictate our sense of self-worth, we give away our power. We allow external factors to define us, instead of embracing our own sense of identity and purpose.
But when we believe in ourselves and our abilities, ***we can accomplish amazing things.***

Addiction

Addiction, a sly and cunning thief
stealing joy and peace like a malignant chief
it starts with a harmless taste
but soon takes over with breakneck haste.

The euphoria it brings, a tempting lure
it's a grip on the mind, hard to endure
a prison of one's own making
a cycle of craving, taking and breaking.

The substance becomes the centre of life
causing endless struggles, pain and strife
it tears apart family and friends
and leaves a trail of destruction that never ends.

Breaking free from addiction, a daunting task
but possible with support, courage and faith to ask.
the road to recovery, long and hard
but worth it to regain what was marred.

Let us lend a helping hand
and understand that addiction is not in one's command
With love, compassion and empathy
we can help break the chains of this melody.

The Problem Is You

I thought it would be different, the second and the third. The times we've started over, the times I have forgiven.
I tell myself things will be different, that the pain you caused would stop. But now I start to wonder if you're capable of love.

Perhaps the problem is me, do I just annoy you that much that the world seems so dark.

No – the problem is you and only you!

You are the destruction of life and joy.

Me? I am the survivor, free from your abuse. I get to move on, live my life away from the clutches of your destruction.

Trapped

Silent tears fall
unseen, unheard
a heart that's breaking
without a word.

Trapped in a cage
of the mind's own making
a prisoner of thoughts
that are suffocating.

The pain is real
though its hidden away
no-one knows the struggle
of getting through each day.

So, if you see someone
who seems lost in thought
be kind, be patient
for battles may be fought.

For those who silently hurt
and feel trapped in their mind
may you find your way out
and a peace that's kind.

Sounds of Darkness

When despair for life grows and I wake in the night.
I wander aimlessly listening to the sounds of the darkness.
A fox screams and owls soar as I lay my head back down to rest.

I wonder when my mind would be free, free to dream, free to imagine what life would be like without PTSD. Free to stop reliving that moment it all changed.

I start to count sheep as I slowly drift back to sleep, drowning out the sounds of the darkness, dreaming about what tomorrow may bring.

Grudges

Don't hold a grudge, it's not worth the pain
let go of anger, release the chain
forgive and forget, move on with grace
choose love and kindness in every case.

Holding a grudge is a heavy weight
it only brings bitterness and hate
it's better to rise above the fray
then let resentment lead the way.

Life is too short to waste on strife
choose to live with joy and light
let go of grudges, be free to soar
and let love guide you ever more.

Stage 4 PTSD

The body shakes, the mind races
memories flood, emotions take their places
the trauma of the past, it lingers on
invisible wounds that can't be gone.

Stage 4 PTSD, a battle within
a fight that's fought with no guarantee of win
the triggers are many, the flashbacks intense
each day a struggle, every moment a test.

But amidst the chaos, hope still prevails
the strength to endure, the courage to unveil
the power within, to face the fear
to heal the wounds, to shed a tear.

So, hold on tight, warrior of light
your journey is hard, but you're not alone in this fight.
together we stand, united we thrive
to conquer the trauma and come out alive.

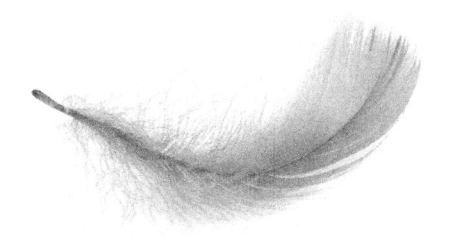

'Never Give Up'

Scars

My scars tell a story, one of battles won and lost
of moments of courage and times when I paid the cost
they show the world my strength, my resilience, my might
and remind me every day that I have survived the fight.

Each scar marks a moment, a memory of my past
of the struggles that I faced, and how I overcame at last
they're a reminder of the lessons that I learned along the way
of the people who supported me and helped me through each day.

So, I wear my scars with pride, for they are part of me
a symbol of my journey and all that I have come to be
they tell a story of survival, of hope and of grace
and I am grateful for each and every one, in their own special place.

Deadly Substance

In the depths of the woods
a deadly substance lurks
a potion so potent
it can make even the strongest man shirk.

Poison, oh poison
a venomous delight
it creeps into your system
and weakens you with all its might.

From the tips of your toes
to the crown on your head
it spreads like wildfire
until you're lying there dead.

Oh, the power of poison
a force to be reckoned with
it can bring down a kingdom
and leave nothing but a myth

So, beware of this poison
and steer clear of its grasp
for once it takes hold
there's no escaping its deadly clasp.

A Life Not Yet Lived

Grief for a life not yet lived
a sorrow that cannot comprehend
a dream unfulfilled, a hope deceived
a future that was never shared.

A life cut short before it began
a story that will never unfold
a heart that beats for an unknown plan
a tale that will never be told.

The pain of loss is hard to bear
when there's no memory to hold
a void that cannot be repaired
a hurt that cannot be consoled.

But though this life was never lived
it leaves a mark upon our hearts
a love that will always be missed
a bond that never truly departs.

So, let us cherish what we have
and hold our loved ones close and dear
for life is fragile and it can pass
and leave us with only tears.

Sorry

We are sorry for the hurt we caused
for the times we left you feeling lost
we didn't mean to cause you pain
and we know we can't turn back the clock again.

We are sorry for the words we said
for the tears that were left unshed
we didn't mean to be so unkind
and we know we can't erase it from your mind.

We are sorry for the mistakes we made
for the trust that we betrayed
we didn't mean to let you down
and we know we can't just turn it all around.

But we promise to learn from our past
to be better people, make amends that last
we will work to earn your trust
and we hope that forgiveness is a must

So, please know that we are truly sorry
and we hope that you can find it in your heart to
forgive us wholly.

Fear

When fear creeps in, it's hard to ignore
but you must be brave and not abort
the challenges that life throws your way
for they will make you stronger day by day.

It's ok to feel scared and unsure
to doubt yourself and feel insecure
but don't let that fear consume your soul
take a deep breath and take control.

Face your fears with courage and might
don't let them hold you back from the light
embrace the unknown and take a chance
you may be surprised with outcomes dance.

So, don't be afraid to step out of your shell
to take a risk and break through your spell
for you have the power to conquer and soar
and become the person you've been longing for.

Secrets Lie

Behind closed doors, what secrets lie, what mysteries unfold, hidden from the eye.
We often wonder what happens inside, but the truth may be something we cannot abide.

Innocence Lost

A child's eyes, so pure and bright
should never have to face such fright
but behind closed doors, a different scene
a nightmare that no child should have to dream.

Hands that should have held with love
instead leave bruises, a painful shove
words that should be kind and sweet
are replaced with threats that make hearts skip a beat.

Innocence lost; a childhood stolen
by those who should have protected, not broken
but hope remains, a light in the dark
for those who have been hurt, a new start.

Let us stand together to break the silence
to give a voice to those who suffered in silence.
to create a world where every child is safe and loved
where their dreams can soar, like a dove.

The Road Ahead

When the road ahead seems long and winding
and the journey feels too rough to bear
remember that the toughest times in life
are the ones that truly test our mettle and our care.

For it's in those moments of darkness
that we find courage to shine
to rise above doubts and fears
and to claim what's rightfully mine.

So, never give up, dear friend
for the power lies within your heart
to chase your dreams and reach your goals
and to make a brand-new start.

Believe in yourself and your abilities
and hold your head up high
for the road may be tough, but with faith and hope
you can conquer the world and touch the sky.

Behind Closed Doors

Behind closed doors, a secret hides
a darkness that nobody sees outside
a place where pain and fear reside
where dignity and hope slowly subside.

Behind closed doors, a voice is silenced
a cry for help that is never heard
a life of misery that is endured
a love that is twisted and obscured.

Behind closed doors, a heart is broken
a soul that is shattered and torn
a body that is bruised and beaten
a spirit that is weakened and forlorn.

Behind closed doors, the truth is hidden
a reality that is hard to believe
a tragedy that is hard to conceive
a horror that nobody should live.

Behind closed doors, a victim suffers
alone and afraid without a voice
but we can make a choice
to listen, to care, to act and to rejoice.

Behind closed doors, a hope can bloom
a light that can shine in the dark
a hand that can reach out and embrace
on a journey towards a new start.

Believe in Yourself

Don't let the world tell you that you're not enough, you are already everything you need to be. ***Believe in yourself*** trust in your abilities and know that you have the power to create a life that is ***fulfilling and meaningful.***

Overdose

Overdose, a thief in the night
stealing futures, stealing life
a darkness that consumes the soul
leaving loved ones with an endless hole.

It starts with pain, with hurt and fear
and soon the addiction draws near
a temporary relief, a moment of peace
but in the end, it's the addiction that's released.

The body cries out, it begs for more
but the mind is numb it can't keep score
and in that moment, everything fades
leaving behind shattered lives and broken shades.

But there is hope, there's a way out
with love and support, with a helping hand,
we can fight this thief, this deadly bout
and reclaim the futures that we had planned.

So, let us stand together, let us fight
for those we've lost, for those in sight
and with every step, with every stride
let us remember those who've died.

Precious Gem

A friend is like a precious gem
their worth can never be measured or known
a bond that cannot be broken
a love that cannot be shown.

But when that friend is suddenly gone
the heart is left shattered and torn
memories of laughter and joy
new replaced with pain and mourn.

The emptiness they leave behind
is too much for the heart to bear
the tears that fall are a testament
to the love that they did share.

But even though they're no longer here
their memory will live on
for they'll always hold a special place
in the heart of the one left behind.

Hiding

In the silence of the night
I hide the truth and pain from sight
my heart beats with a heavy weight
as I try to escape this endless state.

The words I hold back, the tears I fight
all to keep up the façade so bright
but deep inside, the pain remains
and the truth seeks to break its chains.

I fear the judgement, the shame and blame
so, I bury my feelings, my heart and my shame
but in the end, it's only myself I deceive
as the truth and pain refuse to leave.

So, I embrace the vulnerability, the rawness inside
and open-up to those who by my side abide
for only then can I find the strength to heal
and let go of the pain I've concealed.

We Are Not Alone

In the midst of pain and heartbreak, it is also important to remember that we are not alone. There are people who care about us, who love us, and who want nothing more than to see us happy and thriving. It is in these moments that we should lean on our friends, family and support systems, and allow them to lift us up when we cannot do it ourselves.

Emptiness

There's a sadness within me
a weight that drags me down
it feels like a heavy burden
that I can't seem to shake or drown.

It's a feeling of emptiness
that tugs at my very core
a sense of loneliness and sorrow
that I've never felt before.

I try to push it aside
and think of happier things
but the sadness just persists
and my heart still aches and stings.

I hope that one day soon
the sadness will fade away
and I'll be left with peace and joy
to brighten up my day.

Negative Thoughts

Darkness creeps in like a thief in the night
negative thoughts and feelings take flight
they whisper in your ear, bringing you down
until you're lost and can't be found.

The weight of the world feels like too much to bear
and you can't escape the grip of despair
the voices in your head won't let you be
no matter how hard you try to break free.

But know you are not alone in this fight
there's a glimmer of hope in the darkest night
reach out your hand, don't be afraid
together we'll face the demons that invade.

For every negative thought, there's a positive one
and for every dark cloud, is a silver lining
so, don't give up, keep moving forward
and soon enough, you'll find your reward.

Intimacy

Intimacy once felt like a warm embrace
a safe haven, a loving place
but all that changed in a single night
when my body was taken, my soul took flight.

Now every touch feels like a threat
a reminder of what I can't forget
the closeness that once brought me joy
now fills me with fear, a broken toy.

I long to feel love's sweet release
to let go of pain and find some peace
but the scars are deep, the wounds still raw
and trust in something I cannot restore.

So, I'll take my time and heal my heart
and pray that one day a new love will start
until then, I'll hold myself tight
and keep fighting for a better night.

'The very least you can do in your life is figure out what you hope for'

Homeless

Homeless and alone
they wander the streets
hoping for a place to call home
and a warm bed to sleep.

It's a Trap

The cards are dealt, the dice are rolled
the rush of the game, the feeling bold
but soon it turns, the luck runs dry
the addiction takes hold, you can't deny.

The thrill of the win, the high it brings
the thought of more, the siren sings
but then it fades, the money's gone
the pain sets in, you're all alone.

The cycle repeats, the hope is strong
the urge to bet, the need to belong
but it's a trap, a downward spiral
the addiction grips, it's hard to stifle.

So, heed the warning, the risk is real
the toll it takes, the way you feel
seek help, a way out, there is a choice
break the chains, regain your voice.

Narcissist

Living with a narcissist can be tough
their ego often feels like it's enough
their needs, take priority over all
and it can feel like you're hitting a wall.

They demand constant attention and praise
and criticism is met with angry displays
their charm can be alluring at first
but soon their selfishness becomes a curse.

Gaslighting and manipulation are their tools
leaving you feeling like a fool
they twist your words and play mind games
leaving you wondering who is to blame.

It's hard to break free from their grasp
but remember, you deserve more than this rasp
seek support, take steps to heal
and one day the narcissists power will repeal.

Night Terrors

In the midnight hour, when all is still and dark
the haunted dreams come creeping in
stark whispers of the past and shadows of the dead
filling your mind with fear and dread.

Silent screams echo through the halls
as you wander through deserted walls
a ghostly presence lingers in the air
as you try to escape from its snare.

The night terrors grip you tight
as you struggle to find the light
but even in the safety of your bed
the ghosts of the past still fill your head.

Haunted dreams and silent screams
a never-ending cycle of terror it seems
but take heart, my friend and do not fear
for with each dawn, a new day is near.

Mental Torture

Mental torture, a pain unseen
a battle fought within the mind
a constant war, a vicious scheme
a struggle that's both cruel and unkind.

It's a fight that knows no end
a darkness that clouds the soul
a fear that cannot befriend
a wound that never can be whole.

It eats away at your very core
leaving scars that no-one can see
it's a pain that you cannot ignore
a burden that's never set free.

It's a silent killer, a thief of joy
a monster that never sleeps
a demon that no-one can destroy
a secret that nobody keeps.

Mental torture, a living hell
a war that's fought in silence
a pain that no words can tell
a struggle that needs no violence.

Treatment

Radiotherapy and chemotherapy
strains that we must bear
fighting cancer with all our might
with hope and prayer.

The radiation beams pierce through
targeting the cancer cells
destroying them one by one
as our body swells.

Chemotherapy is no easy feat
with side effects that take a toll
but we endure the nausea and fatigue
to save our precious soul.

It's a journey that's long and tough
but we're not alone in this fight
our loved ones and healthcare team
make everything feel right.

So, don't lose hope, don't give up
keep pushing through the pain
for in the end, we'll emerge victorious
and our strength will never wain.

Love

Love is a force that fills the heart with light
a feeling that makes everything feel right
It shines like a beacon through the darkest night
and makes the world a wondrous sight.

Love is a song that makes the heart sing
a melody that brings joy in everything
it lifts the soul on angels' wings
and makes the heart take flight and soar like kings.

Love is like a flower that blooms in the heart
a fragrance that lingers and never departs
it brings forth beauty that never falls apart
and fills the world with endless art.

Love is a miracle that makes life divine
a gift that brings happiness and makes us shine
it fills the heart with a warmth that's divine
and makes us believe in magic that's truly fine.

Age UK

Growing old is a privilege
a gift that not all receive
yet, it can be a challenge
to make the most of what we achieve.

Age UK is an organisation
that helps the elderly thrive
it offers support and guidance
so that they can truly come alive.

With Age UK by our side
we can age with grace and pride
for growing old is a journey
that we need not take alone
with Age UK, we have a community
and a place to call our own.

So, let us cherish every moment
and embrace what's yet to come
with Age UK's help and guidance
growing old can be a lot of fun.

Unplanned

Unplanned and unexpected
a life now growing inside
a wave of emotions
and a rollercoaster ride.

Fear and uncertainty
mixed with hope and love
a choice to be made
with no guidance from above.

No matter the decision
support and care are key
for those facing unwanted pregnancy
compassion is what they need to see.

Little Fighters

Amidst the beeping of machines and the sterile smell of the ward
lies a group of little fighters, their spirits never floored
they battle every moment, with strength beyond their years
their courage and resilience, bringing hope and wiping tears.

Their tiny bodies weakened, but their will to live is strong
their families by their side, praying they will pull through the long
days and nights they spend, in this foreign sterile land.
their futures uncertain, but they fight with all they can.

The nurses and the doctors, work tirelessly each day
to help these little warriors, keep the illness at bay
the parents watch with bated breath, as their child fights on
their hearts filled with love and hope, that their child will overcome.

So, let us remember, these brave children fighting for life
and send them all our love and strength, as they endure this strife
may they find the courage deep within, to keep fighting strong
for they are the true heroes, and their spirit will live on.

Head vs Heart

In the depths of my mind, a battle rage on
a war between my heart and my head, long gone
my fears and doubts they tear me apart
a fight that seems to never depart.

But I am a warrior strong and brave
I stand tall, determined to be saved
from the darkness that threatens to consume me
I rise, stronger than I ever thought I could be.

With each passing day, I learn to fight
to conquer the demons that haunt me at night
my scars are proof of battles won
and I know that I am not yet done

For though the war may never truly end
I will stand my ground, and hope will transcend
the battles within, they make me who I am
and I will survive, for I know that I can.

Sorrow

Losing a baby is a pain beyond measure
a sorrow that cuts like a blade of a sharp razor
the emptiness that follows is hard to describe
a void that no words can truly circumscribe

Unanswered questions and shattered dreams
a future that vanished like a thin steam
a love that was felt, but never seen
a life that was hoped, but never been.

The heartache is real, the tears are true
the pain is something only a few can construe
but know that you are not alone in this pain
there are others who share it, who feel the same.

Take comfort in the memories that you hold
true moments shared, the love that was told
for though your baby may be gone from sight
their spirit and love with forever shine bright.

Triangle

My heart is torn in two
between the love of me and you
and the other one that came along
and stole my heart with his sweet song.

I try to choose between the two
but my heart is so confused
one brings laughter one brings peace
but with each, my love will never cease.

I know I must make a choice
and silence one of the inner voices
but how can I let go of love so true
and choose just one to start anew.

Stuck in this love triangle
my hearts caught in a tangled wrangle
but I know someday I'll find my way
and choose the one with whom I'll stay.

Lotus Flower

The years will never take away your chance to start anew.
Like the lotus flower, you too, have the **strength to bloom** out of the darkness into **the light of the sun.**

Past Mistakes

Past mistakes haunt my mind
memories of errors unkind
regret fills my heart
as I wish for a fresh start.

I replay the moments in my head
wishing I could go back instead
but time marches on
and the chance is gone.

I must learn to forgive
and let go, so I can live
for dwelling on the past
will just make the pain last.

So, I take a deep breath
and put past mistakes to rest
for tomorrow is a new day
and a chance to find a better way.

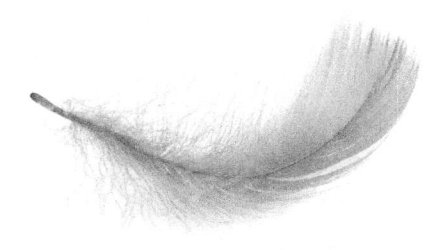

'Poetry flows from pen like rain falls from the sky,
If only the words I write, could wash away your pain'

Friendships

Friendships that last through thick and thin
are the ones that truly win
with laughter, tears and all in between
our bond remains strong, forever keen.

Through trials and hardships, we stand by each other
with unwavering support like no other
we lift each other up when we fall
and celebrate the good times, big and small.

Our memories together will never fade
as we journey through life's winding maze
with each passing day, we grow close still
forever grateful for friendships that fill.

So, here's to the friends who've stood the test of time
who make our world brighter, like sunshine
we cherish you more than words can say
forever grateful, come what may.

Change

Change is a constant in life
it can be challenging, but it can also be rife
we all face moments when we must adjust
and leave behind what we thought was just.

Change can be daunting and scary
but it's necessary, and it can be quite merry
embrace it with an open heart
and you'll find a whole new start.

Making changes can be hard
but it's not something to disregard
it can lead to growth and new beginnings
and help us find our new true meaning.

So, when life presents a chance to change
don't be afraid to rearrange
embrace the journey and take the leap
and you'll find a new path to take.

Anorexia

When I was a child
I could see the food on my plate
pushing it around
I couldn't stomach the taste

One mouthful I try
the anxiety builds
another one I try
the sickness begins

The food has control
my anorexia wins
I'm losing weight
my body now thins

But there's hope in sight
as food loses its power
the strength in me
means the food I can devour.

Frustration

Frustration, oh frustration
you weigh heavy on my mind
a constant source of irritation
a feeling that's hard to unwind.

You come when I least expect it
and linger for far too long
a feeling of being restricted
a sense that everything's gone wrong

I try to shake you off
to push you far away
but you cling on like a stubborn cough
refusing to let me have my say.

So, I'll take a deep breath
and face you with a smile
I may not conquer you just yet
but I'll make it all worthwhile

For frustration, oh frustration
you may be a constant fight
but I'll keep pushing and striving
until I finally see the light.

Women

In a world that's often cruel
women are treated like a tool
their worth is measured by their looks
their voices silenced by the crooks.

They're told to be quiet and demure
to never speak out and endure
their bodies are objectified
their minds and hearts left untried.

But women are strong and wise
with voices that can reach the skies
we must stand up for their rights
and let them shine in all their might.

For a world that treats women well
is a world where we can all excel
let's lift them up and let them be
the powerful souls that we need to see.

The Storms of Life

Through the storms of life, I have stood strong
and though I've been knocked down, I'll rise before too long
my trials and tribulations have left scars
but I refuse to let them define who I am.

For I am powerful, I am strong
and I will rise above all the wrongs
I will not let my past dictate my state
for I am the master of my own fate.

I'll rise each day, like the sun
and I'll keep rising, until my race is run
for I am a fighter, a warrior, a queen
and I will rise above everything.

So, let the storms rage on, let the winds blow
for I am still rising, and I'll never let go
I'll conquer all, I'll surpass all strife
for I am still rising, still rising in life.

Shattered Glass

Mental health is like shattered glass
fragile and delicate, it can easily pass
one moment you're whole, the next you're not
a single crack can change your whole plot.

The pieces scatter, hard to put back
it's easy to feel like you're under attack
the sharp edges cut deep inside
it's hard to escape from the pain you hide.

But just like glass, you can be mended
with time and care, your wounds can be tended
the cracks may still show, but that's okay
you're still beautiful in your own unique way.

So, if you're feeling broken and lost
remember that you're not alone at any cost
reach out for help, don't hide in the dark
you're stronger than you think, and you'll leave your mark.

I'm Fine

I'm fine, I say with a smile
but deep down I'm in denial
I'm hurting, I'm struggling, I'm lost
but the words *I'm fine* come at a cost.

I don't want to burden; I don't want to bring down
so, I keep up the façade, I wear the crown
of the person who's got it all together
when I'm fighting stormy weather.

I wish I could be honest; I wish I could share
but the fear of judgement, the fear of being a
burden is always there
so, I'll keep saying *I'm fine* for a while
but are we really fine, or is it just a lie?

Hope

Hope is a light that shines so bright
it fills our hearts with warmth and light
when life brings darkness to our door
it's hope that helps us to endure.

It's like a seed that's planted deep
that grows and blossoms, even in sleep
it gives us strength to face each day
and chase our fears and doubts away.

Hope is a friend that's always near
to dry our tears and calm our fears
it lifts us up when we fall down
and helps us find a brighter crown.

So, let us hold onto this grace
and let it guide us to a better place
for with hope, we can truly soar
and find the joy we're looking for.

Seeking Help

Age UK
https://www.ageuk.org.uk/
Help and support for the older generation

Andys Man Club
https://andysmanclub.co.uk/
Men's mental health charity

Beat Eating Disorders
https://www.beateatingdisorders.org.uk/
Advice on eating disorders.

Cancer Research UK
https://www.cancerresearchuk.org/
Cancer diagnosis help and advice

Citizens Advice
https://www.citizensadvice.org.uk/
Financial help and advice.

Gamble Aware
https://www.begambleaware.org/
Advice and support for gamblers

Mind
https://www.mind.org.uk/
Mental health charity

SANDS
https://www.sands.org.uk/
Child and infant loss charity

Shelter
https://england.shelter.org.uk/
Homeless help and support

Thank you for taking the time to read this book, I hope you enjoyed it as much as I enjoyed writing it. I hope it offered some help and hope to all those that need it. Just know that it's okay to talk!

Please feel free to contact me through Instagram
@mrsharverson15
Facebook: Michelle Harverson LLB (hons)

Other books available to purchase on Amazon.

A Prescription of Poetry – Life in a Pharmacy

A Prescription of Poetry – Mind, Body & Soul

A Prescription of Poetry – Faith, Friendship & Forgiveness.

Unspoken – Poetry and Prose.